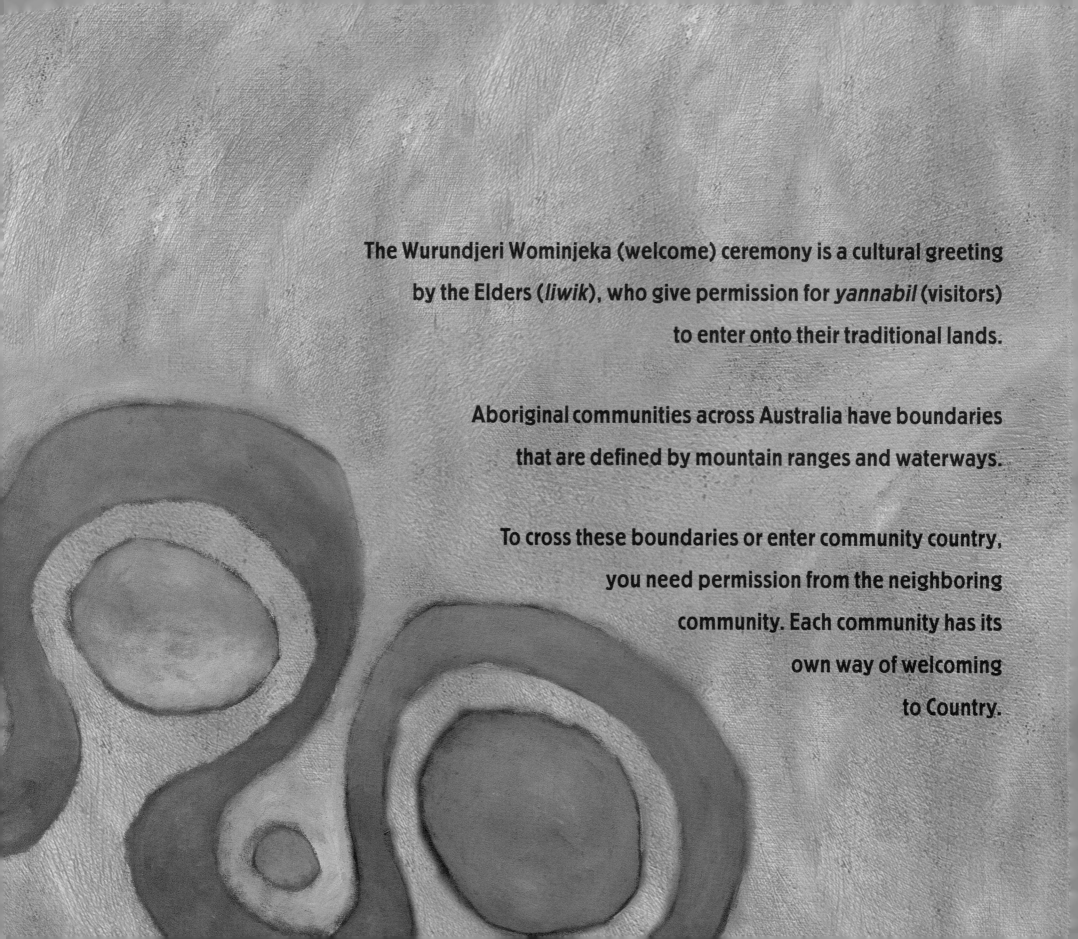

The Wurundjeri Wominjeka (welcome) ceremony is a cultural greeting by the Elders (*liwik*), who give permission for *yannabil* (visitors) to enter onto their traditional lands.

Aboriginal communities across Australia have boundaries that are defined by mountain ranges and waterways.

To cross these boundaries or enter community country, you need permission from the neighboring community. Each community has its own way of welcoming to Country.

WELCOME WORDS
BY AUNTY JOY MURPHY

Welcome to Country

WITH ILLUSTRATIONS
BY LISA KENNEDY

CANDLEWICK PRESS

Wominjeka
Wurundjeri
balluk yearmenn
koondee bik.

**Welcome to the traditional lands
of the Wurundjeri people.**

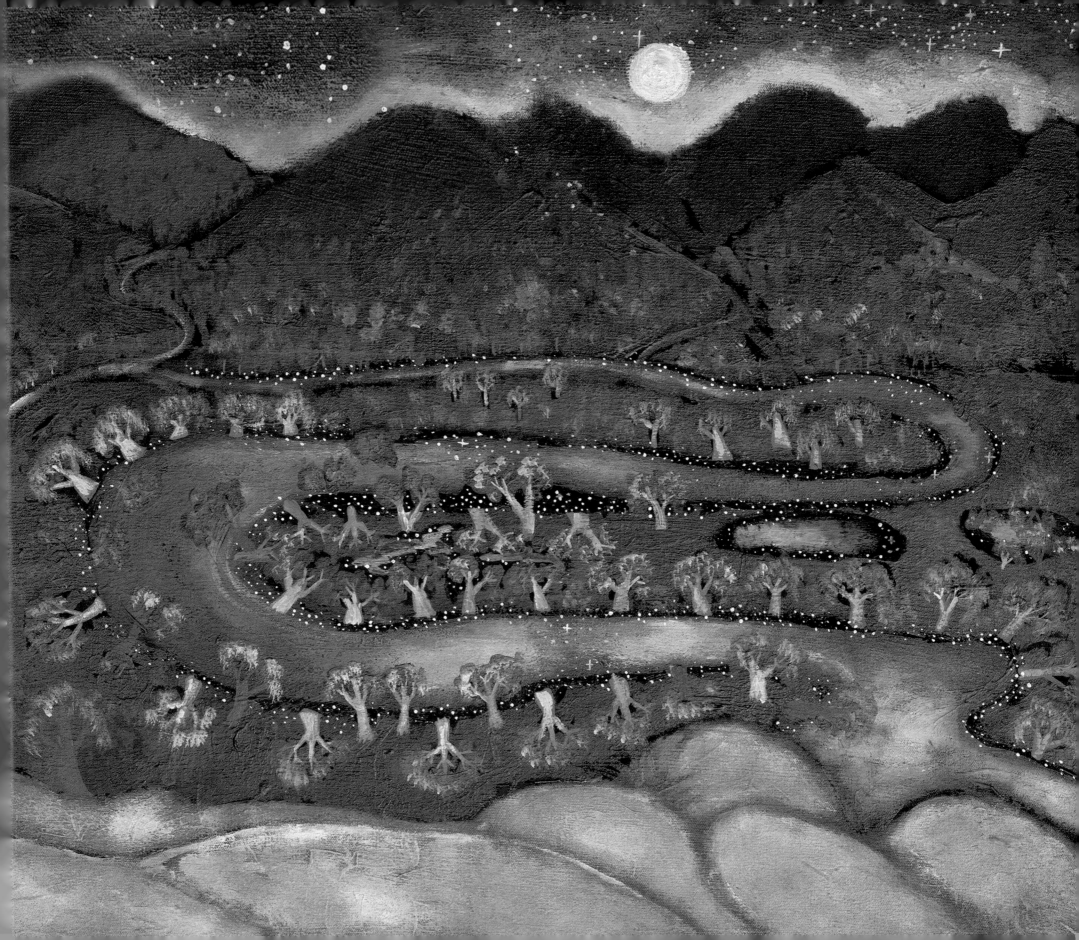

Our ancestors left their mark on the land
for us to follow in their footsteps.
We have a presence on this earth
through the spirits of our ancestors.

We respectfully acknowledge our elders and the community
of this land and all elders and communities
of this continent and neighboring islands.
We thank them for their courage, strength,
integrity, and values.

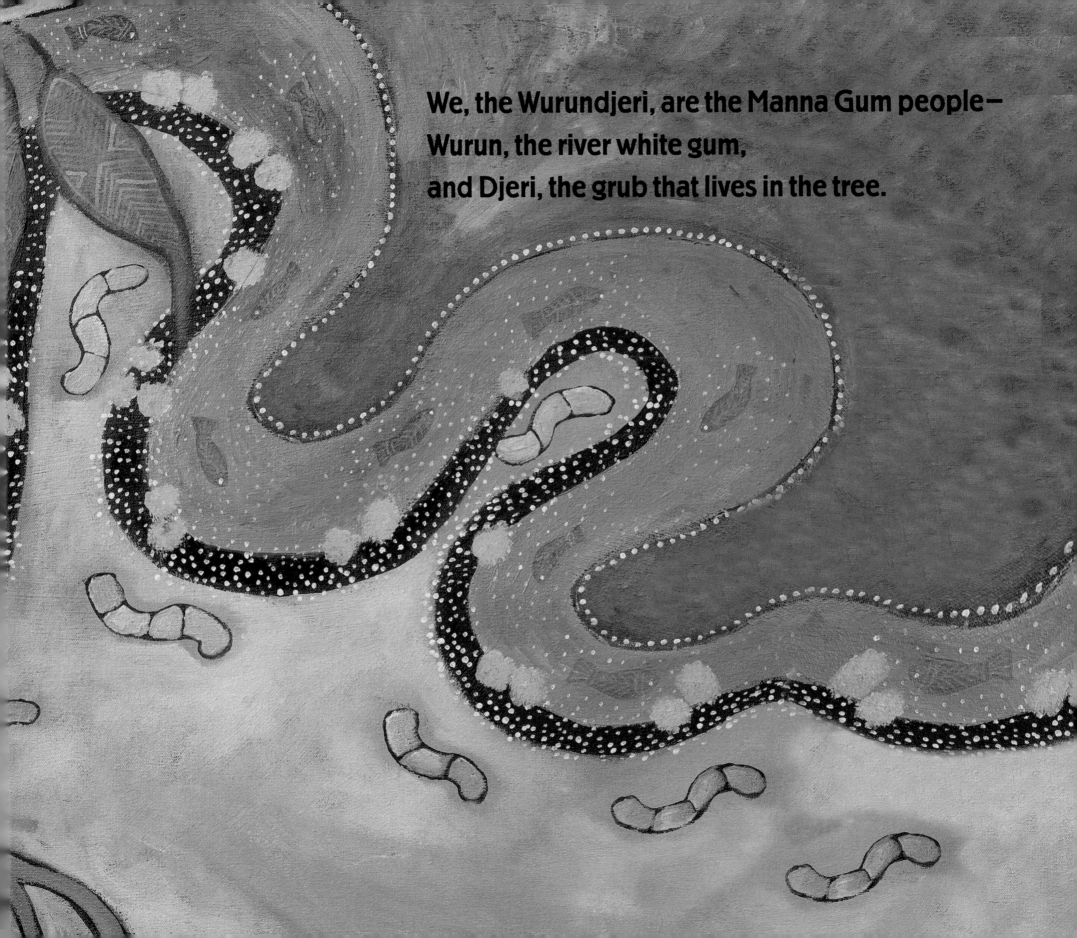

We, the Wurundjeri, are the Manna Gum people—
Wurun, the river white gum,
and Djeri, the grub that lives in the tree.

Bunjil the eagle is our creator spirit.
Bunjil created man, woman, and child from the land.

Bunjil created the birds,
the animals, the mountains, the rivers.
Bunjil created all things natural
from the land.
Bunjil watches over the indelible
footprints of our ancestors
on this land.

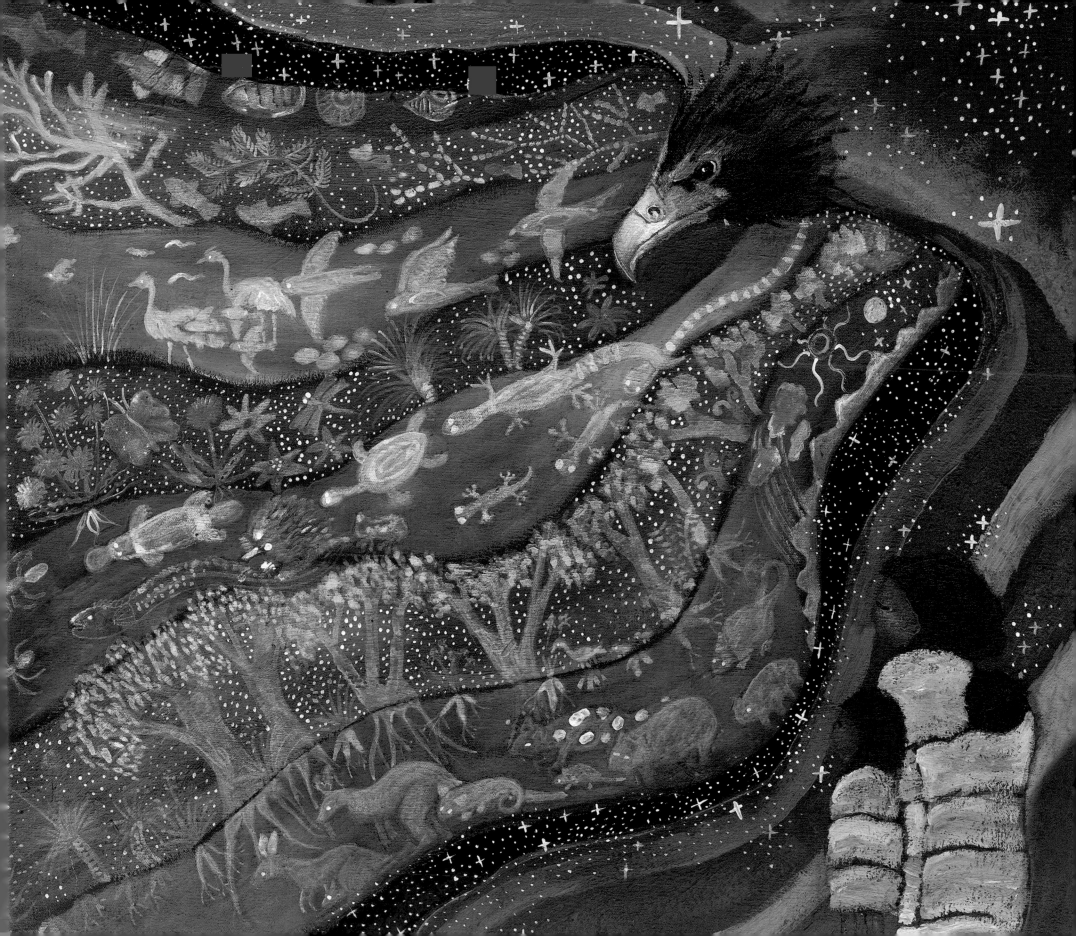

We invite you to take a leaf from the branches of the white river gum. If you accept a leaf, and we hope you do, it means you are welcome to everything, from the tops of the trees to the roots of the earth. But you must take from this land only what you can give back.

We thank you,
for you have now
joined with us
to pay respect
to the spirit of
our ancestors,
who have
nurtured this
land for
thousands
of years.

We are part of the land, and the land is part of us.
We feel the roots of this land beneath the soles of our bare feet.

This is where we come from.
Our language is the Woiwurrung Ngulu.

Wominjeka Wurundjeri balluk yearmenn koondee bik.

Welcome to the traditional lands of the Wurundjeri people.

Welcome to Country.

Jarlo: Your £2.6d gave us kids

a permanent place to live.

Mum: Your stamina and determination

kept us strong and disciplined.

You taught me the gift of generosity and pride in our belonging.

This is Blackfellas' place. Come into our humble abode

and share what we have been given.

J. M.

For the Wurundjeri community – ancestors,

Elders, children, and future generations

L. K.

In memory of Joshua Robert Hardy

JOY MURPHY WANDIN AO is the Senior Aboriginal Elder of the Wurundjeri people of Melbourne and the surrounding area. We show respect for her and other Elders by calling them Aunty or Uncle.

Aunty Joy has had numerous government appointments, including as a member of the Equal Opportunity Commission of Victoria and of the Anti-Discrimination Tribunal. She is a storyteller and a writer and is passionate about using story to bring people together and as a conduit for understanding Aboriginal culture.

LISA KENNEDY is a descendant of the Trawlwoolway people on the northeast coast of Tasmania. She was born in Melbourne and as a child lived close to the Maribyrnong River. Here she experienced the gradual restoration of the natural river environment alongside cultural regeneration and reclamation. Through sense of place, she feels connected to the Wurundjeri country and all that entails – the water, the land, the animals, and the ancestors. The experience of loss and reclamation is embedded in her work.

First U.S. edition 2018

Library of Congress Catalog Card Number pending
ISBN 978-0-7636-9499-9

17 18 19 20 21 22 APS 10 9 8 7 6 5 4 3 2 1

Printed in Humen, Dongguan, China

This book was typeset in Berliner Grotesk.
The illustrations were created with acrylic on canvas.

Candlewick Press
99 Dover Street
Somerville, Massachusetts 02144

visit us at www.candlewick.com